Breath Marks

Breath Marks

Haiku to Read in the Dark

Gary Hotham

Canon Press

MOSCOW, IDAHO

Gary Hotham, *Breath Marks: Haiku to Read in the Dark*

© 1999 by Gary Hotham
Published by Canon Press, P.O. Box 8741, Moscow, ID 83843
800-488-2034 / www.canonpress.org

05 04 03 02 01 00 99   9 8 7 6 5 4 3 2 1

Cover design by Paige Atwood Design, Moscow, ID

Printed in the United States of America.

ISBN: 1-885767-58-7

Contents

Why Poetry? 9
First Lines
    fog 17
    wild geese 18
    shade trees on both sides 19
    coffee 20
    night comes 21
    more darkness 22
    all 23
    this way that way 24
    still shadows 25
    picking up the shells 26
    the heat 27
    letting 28
    my wife still asleep 29
    loud wind 30
    stepping out of the wind 31
    pond ripples 32
    morning quiet 33
    to hear them 34
    my move 35
    another day of snow 36

home early 37
every way 38
as far as the light goes 39
part of 40
not much afternoon left 41
the way back 42
last night's snow 43
music two centuries old 44
rest stop 45
the wind 46
late in the day sunlight 47
spring wind 48
distant thunder 49
more coffee made 50
green light 51
snow now rain 52
third day of rain 53
autumn rain 54
back water 55
below the glass 56
night snow 57
through 58
on our way back 59
last night's 60
raspberries in season 61

beginning rain 62

the park bench 63

on my birthday 64

up late 65

the library book 66

no place 67

no hurry in the wind 68

outside the door 69

someone else's 70

our daughter runs back 71

soft rain 72

I lean 73

at the bus stop 74

the cough of my wife 75

deserted tennis court 76

quietly 77

each lull 78

three caws 79

sipping the soup 80

this summer night 81

the sound they make 82

partly fog 83

waiting up 84

a pile of orange peelings 85

around our feet 86

their last sound 87
yesterday's paper 88
the newborn yawns 89
hand to hand 90
she comes back 91
one mirror for everyone 92
time to go 93
shadow 94
early in the night 95
before the dew is off 96
in both hands 97

Why Haiku? 99
Endnotes 104
On Location 107
Acknowledgments 111

Why Poetry?

He has made his wonders to be remembered.
   — Psalm 111:4a

In all of creation, one of the greatest possessions we have is our language. Our words not only tell us what we see but what we think: "And out of the ground the Lord God formed every beast of the field and every bird of the sky, and brought them to the man to see what he would call them; and whatever the man called a living creature, that was its name. And the man gave names to all the cattle, and to the birds of the sky, and to every beast of the field . . ." (Genesis 2:19–20 NASB). Just as Adam named the living creatures, the poet names the significant things and the important events of life, because life has meaning, because words have meaning by the grace of God.

Of course the idea that words are not all that powerful or important is common. It is intriguing to think about why we try to play down the power of words—with other words no less.

(1) We have all heard and probably said: Sticks and stones may break my bones but words will never hurt me (is there a saying like this in all cultures/languages or just English?). In most cases it's probably a statement of bravado. We all know how much words hurt and continue to hurt long after the sticks and stones. Remembering the unpleasant words someone said about us can cause us pain again, but remembering the blows of stick and stones will not cause the same physical pain.

(2) And of course there is that other very popular canard: A picture is worth a thousand words (sometimes qualified with

a "can be"!). Just think of all the pictures that have left you in total ignorance when a thousand words would have given some understanding of the scene. Living in a world of just pictures would be something like living in a foreign country when one doesn't know the language. Obviously seeing is a way of learning and understanding, but knowing the language would certainly deepen and expand one's understanding more quickly.

But why read or write poetry? Well, because poetry lets the writer do something with our language that other forms do not. And that something special is the energy inherent in the words and their arrangement. For example, we see a river flowing by. The various scientists could describe in very precise chemical terms the formula for the water and the pollutants in the water, or list and describe all the living organisms in the water, or the plants growing in the water or on the riverbank, or the type of rocks and soil that the water flows over. The geographer could describe the effect the river has had on the land or where it comes from or is going to. The anthropologist could describe what part the river has in forming the cultures of the people living near it. The historian could narrate the history along the river of peoples, towns, battles, bridges, disastrous floods, and droughts. But a poem about the river would use words that give some sort of delight or pleasure or excitement or insight or wisdom or feeling or wonder. Of course, we might find this in the writings of the chemist, biologist, geographer, or historian, but not as a primary focus. For them, it's not in how the words tell but what the words tell. In poetry, it's how the words are combined that's most important for the power and deep effect of the poem upon the reader. My intent and my hope would be that the poems in this book would make us remember the wonder of God's creation and also

let us maintain focus on truth, beauty, and
goodness in all its manifestations:

> Finally, brethren,
> whatever is true,
> whatever is honorable,
> whatever is right,
> whatever is pure,
> whatever is lovely,
> whatever is of good repute,
> if there is any excellence
> and if anything worthy of praise,
> let your mind dwell on these things.
> (Philippians 4:8)

Gary Hotham
Cheltenham, England
23 January 1999

Breath Marks

fog.
sitting here
without the mountains

wild geese—
the clouds too low
to see them

shade trees on both sides—
the same road
Napoleon took

coffee
in a paper cup—
a long way from home

night comes—
picking up your shoes
still warm

more darkness
more fireflies—
more darkness than fireflies

all
the daylight gone—
her songs
to her granddaughter

this way that way
she tries her hair—
more snow in the wind

still shadows
on still water—
this space blank
for my name

picking up the shells
only her hands have room for—
our daughter ahead of us

the heat
after the rain—
famous men buried here

letting
the dog out—
the stars out

my wife still asleep—
snow piles up
on the steps

loud wind—
the bed unmade
all day

stepping out of the wind
broken glass
underfoot

pond ripples
moving the clouds
moving the sky
moving

morning quiet
snow sticking to this side
of the telephone poles

to hear them
walking more slowly—

leaves falling

my move
their move
morning clouds

another day of snow—
the statue's fingers
broken off

home early—
your empty coat hanger
in the closet

every way
the wind blows—
chrysanthemums

as far as the light goes
my daughter goes
after the firefly

part of
the garden weeded most of
the morning

not much afternoon left—
his dog runs loose
ahead of him

the way back—
every star the naked eye
can see

last night's snow
deer tracks
deer hunter
tracks

music two centuries old—
the color flows
out of the tea bag

rest stop—
in the darkness
the grass stiff with frost

the wind
somewhere else—
bird tracks in a light snow

late in the day sunlight—
the dentist changes
the shape of my tooth

spring wind—
my wife drinks from a cup
we've always had

distant thunder—
the dog's toenails click
against the linoleum

more coffee made
than we drank—
wind off the ocean

green light
from a green bottle
winter morning

snow now rain—
your picture
by mine

third day of rain
the barber cuts my hair
too fast

autumn rain
the statue in the park
turns dark

back water
stillness
here

below the glass
the trout's
lightless eye

night snow—
the house
creaks

through
tall grass taller weeds
her feet wet
her legs wet

on our way back—
nothing left in the sky
of the hawk's circles

last night's snow down river

raspberries in season—
all day I've needed
my hands

beginning rain—
pulling out the bent nail
starting another

the park bench seats two summer dreams

on my birthday
a clear sky before sunrise—
Alexander the Great died younger

up late—
the furnace comes on
by itself

the library book
overdue—
slow falling snow

no place
to hide my hands
the rain begins

no hurry in the wind—
she pulls the hair
from her comb

outside the door
daylight
waits

someone else's
laughter:
spring evening

our daughter runs back—
the shells her hands
can't find room for

soft rain
a bubble
on the water
goes out

I lean
into the soup's steam . . .
snow flurries

at the bus stop
our backs to the wind—
the sunrise changes color

the cough of my wife
louder than the snowstorm
outside . . .

deserted tennis court
wind through the net

quietly
　　the fireworks
　　　　far away . . .

each lull
in the winter wind:
you and I

three caws
and the crow has flown
over

sipping the soup—
the evening light slides down
the bowl's side . . .

this summer night—
she lets the firefly glow
through the cage of her fingers

the sound they make
the sound I make
autumn leaves

partly fog
partly fence
the edge of this road

waiting up—
one hand warms
the other

a pile of orange peelings—
the night watchman
away from his desk

around our feet—
water on its way
to more water

their last sound
before we move on—
the geese outdistance us

yesterday's paper
in the next seat—
the train picks up speed

the newborn yawns—
her hands don't go
far

hand to hand—
the unframed photos
of her life

she comes back—
the ocean drips off
every part of her

one mirror for everyone
the rest stop
restroom

time to go—
the stones we threw
at the bottom of the ocean

shadow
among shadow—
the day begins cold

early in the night—
the stars we can see
the space for more

before the dew is off—
he pulls his son
in the new red wagon

in both hands—
the water she carries
from the ocean

Why Haiku?

> All his art is to recapture a moment
> and seize upon particulars and fasten
> down a contingency.

No, this wasn't written to describe the work
of a haiku poet. It was written by Herbert
Butterfield, the very distinguished British
historian, to describe the work of a histo-
rian.[1] I only came across this quote recently
and found it startling since I have been
interested in history longer than poetry or
writing haiku. The phrase "recapture a
moment" points out an important part of
what I like about the haiku and what I am
trying to do in writing them. So the histo-
rian and the haiku writer are after some of
the same things. It's good to know person-
ally since it says there is a natural affinity

for my interest in both.[2]

Years ago now, but within living memory, three members of the Haiku Society of America, Harold Henderson, William Higginson, and Anita Virgil, put together a definition of the English language haiku.[3] One phrase from that definition expresses well to me the chief goal of a haiku: "the essence of a moment keenly perceived." There is a lot of emotional energy, excitement, and depth in the small events, the brief moments of life. And why not—they are all part of the sweep of history. They are all part of what is significant and important in our lives as God's creatures. The haiku is a great form of poetry with its pinpoint focus for capturing those brief moments in time and re-creating the associated states of being.

I think many have the idea that a haiku is a poem invented by the Japanese consisting of seventeen syllables divided into three lines of 5, 7, 5 and dealing with a subject matter focused on nature. It is an easy form of poetry to teach poetry writing beginners, both young and old, how to write, since the structure is short and simple. Many, many get written, and of course most of them are bad, which doesn't help haiku's reputation. But so are most beginner attempts at poetry, whether it's a sonnet or an epic. If you have read my haiku, you know I don't adhere strictly to those rules. My focus is on perceiving the essence of the moment with the best words and phrases I can think of. That focus becomes my rule. It certainly limits the number of words, although it doesn't arrange them in lines of 5, 7, 5. Too many words would mean more moments and diffuse the sharp edges of a single moment. One line, two lines, three lines, four lines—in most cases three lines does it for me. What's the "does it"? I think the lines, by separating the words and phrases, help intensify them—it gives them some space to expand. At least visually—and even when read aloud—the lines make one pause, giving some space to the sounds. Perhaps the space around a word or between phrases is like water on seeds or boiling water poured on tea leaves. Have you ever wondered how you hear the spaces between words? It's certainly easy enough to see them when the words are written. Is seeing space and hearing space between words the same?

And of course haiku are not just nature poems. There are lots of trees, clouds, wind, snow, and rain in mine, if that is what defines a nature poem. But there are other things in them such as cups of coffee, daughters, famous men, blank forms, soup, dentists, and closets. But even in the ones that look like a nature poem there is us. As far as the materials of the haiku go and its subject matter, all of creation is legitimate. I think the content of a haiku can be thought of in the same way T. S. Eliot describes the materials of the poet at work:

When a poet's mind is perfectly equipped for its work, it is constantly amalgamating disparate experience; the ordinary man's experience is chaotic, irregular, fragmentary. The latter falls in love, or reads Spinoza, and these two experiences have nothing to do with each other or with the noise of the typewriter or the smell of cooking; in the mind of the poet these experiences are always forming new wholes.[4]

I really like how he puts the poet's work as "forming new wholes." That's what I would like my haiku to be. Of course, all of us, in our lives, are forming new wholes with the materials God has given us.

Gary Hotham
24 March 1999
The night NATO started bombing Serbia,
Kosovo, and Montenegro

Endnotes:

[1] Herbert Butterfield, *The Whig Interpretation of History* (London: G. Bell and Sons, Ltd., 1950; first published in 1931) p. 66. And recently Michael D. Welch wrote an insightful essay, "Haiku as History," (*Modern Haiku*, Vol XXIX, No. 1 Winter–Spring 1998 pp. 54–56) in which he points out that the haiku is written in the present tense about something that quickly becomes "a small and meaningful slice of the past."

[2] And here is a great quote I found a couple years ago, putting poetry and history together, from Martin Luther: "How I regret now that I did not read more poets and historians, and that no one taught me them!" It's from his essay written in 1524: "To the Councilmen of All Cities in Germany That They Establish and Maintain Christian Schools." He also thought children should study languages and mathematics and singing and instrumental music. You might be surprised which subject of study he had to spend his time on and called the "devil's filth." I wonder what the real German was for that phrase? Anyway I'll let you discover what field of study it was. The essay I read was in volume four, *Works of Martin Luther*—The Philadelphia Edition (Muhlenberg Press, 1931). The quote was on page 123.

[3] For the whole definition and a lot of the story behind it, check out *A Haiku Path: The Haiku Society of America 1968–1988*, edited by the HSA Twentieth Anniversary Book Committee, (Haiku Society of America, Inc., 1994), pp. 43–85. Two other sources for

this definition, which might be easier to find: *The Haiku Anthology: English Language Haiku by Contemporary American and Canadian Poets* (Anchor Press/Doubleday, 1974) and *The Haiku Anthology: Haiku and Senryu in English* (Fireside Books/ Simon & Schuster, 1986). Both edited by Cor van den Heuvel. And while we are still down in this footnote let me mention a very good book for those who desire a better understanding of the haiku both from its Japanese ancestry and as it has become in English: *The Haiku Handbook: How to Write, Share, and Teach Haiku* (McGraw–Hill Book Company, 1985) written by William J. Higginson with Penny Harter.

[4] From Eliot's essay: "The Metaphysical Poets" first published in the Times Literary Supplement, 20 October 1921 and collected in his *Selected Essays 1917–1932* (Harcourt, Brace and Company, 1932) p. 247.

On Location

If you are like my wife and me, you wait to the very end of the movie for the small bits about where it was filmed. Most movie makers don't provide much for those interested in such information. The information is usually at the very end of the credits, which causes us to be the very last ones out of the theater and gets us strange looks from the people trying to clean up the trash the audience left behind. This is not so much a problem with books. Even when footnotes are at the end of the chapter or end of the book rather than at the bottom of the page, one can, without too much effort, turn to them fairly quickly to discover a bit more about the writer's statements. And many times the movie credits do not give as much information as

I would like—sometimes you have to guess where the movie was filmed from whom they thank—"Thanks to the Our Town Chamber of Commerce for their cooperation. . . ." We are curious to know where the scenery of the fictional locations exists: what town in Vermont did they use for the backdrop of the story set in Maine; what fields in California did they use to film the battle scenes for Gettysburg? It would be better if this information was put closer to the front of the movie credits. And, as I think about it, even better if they could put it in as subtext during the movie. As a matter of fact, most movies could do with a lot more text between scenes and during scenes since so much of the story is lost in the acting. It certainly would improve the film media's moral and intellectual respectability.

This is all preface for a list of places in chronological order I have lived in for months and years at a time. Hopefully it will give the reader some feel for the geography of the haiku in this collection. Place fills a large and important part of our lives and of the haiku:

Westfield, Maine
Orono, Maine
Philadelphia, Pennsylvania
San Angelo, Texas
Misawa, Japan
Laurel, Maryland
Gersthofen, Germany
Scaggsville, Maryland

Acknowledgments

These poems first appeared in the follow-
ing magazines, journals, and anthologies:

Ant Ant Ant Ant Ant; *Anthology of Haiku by
the People of the United States and Canada*
(Japan Air Lines–Tokyo); *Amoskeag*;
Bonsai; *Cicada* (Canada); *Dragonfly*;
En Passant; *Frogpond*; *Gusto*;
Haiku (Canada); *Haiku*; *Haiku Quarterly*;
Haiku Quarterly (England); *Haiku West*;
Hummingbird; *Inkstone*; *Longhouse*; *Mati*;
Mayfly; *Modern Haiku*; *Northeast*;
Spafaswap; *Sunday Clothes*; *Sun–Lotus
Haiku*; *Tamarisk*; *The Beloit Poetry Journal*;
Thistle; *Tweed* (Australia); *Wind Chimes*;
Windless Orchard; *Woodnotes*.